I Can Act Now!

By Alexa Patrick

Copyright © 2025 WonderLab Group LLC
Published by Paw Prints Publishing
A division of Baker & Taylor
Paw Prints Publishing and associated logos are trademarks and/or registered trademarks of Baker & Taylor.
All rights reserved. No part of this book may be reproduced or used in any matter without written permission of the copyright owner except for the use of quotations in a book review.
ISBN: 978-1-2231-8872-0 (paperback)
ISBN: 978-1-2231-8873-7 (reinforced library binding)

Library of Congress Cataloging-in-Publication Data available.

For information about special sales and premium purchases, please contact specialsales@btpubservices.com.
www.PawPrintsPublishing.com
Printed in China

Created and produced by WonderLab Group LLC

Written by Alexa Patrick
Series Consulting Editor: Alexa Patrick
Design by Fan Works Design LLC
Photo research by Annette Kiesow
Project Editor: Angela Modany

Be sure to check with an adult before you begin a new project!

Image credits:
Key: bk=background, Shutterstock = Sh
All illustrations by Lyudmyla Kharlamova/Shutterstock unless otherwise noted.
Cover: SeventyFour/Sh, Luis Louro/Sh, Rawpixel/Sh, Pixel-Shot/Sh, (bk) Natalya Kalyatina/Sh1, 4 (bk): Rawpixel.com/Sh; 2 (bk): jamesteohart/Sh; 3: Frogella/Sh; 5: KelseyJ/Sh; 6 poonsap/Sh; 8 (bk): AlyonaZhitnaya/Sh; 9, 24: Jake May/The Flint Journal/AP; 10: Nate Hovee/Sh; 11: Ververidis Vasilis/Sh; 12: Jacob Boomsma/Sh; 13 (bk): Sichon/Sh; 14-15 (signs): photka/Sh; 14-16 (bk) Poonotsuke/Sh; 16: Lorna Roberts/Sh; 17 (bk): Pixel-Shot/Sh; 18-19: David Prado Perucha/Sh; 20: Molly Riley/UPI/Alamy, 21. 5D Media/Sh; 22: Ben Wehrman/Sh; 23: Dave Coulson Photography/Sh; 25 (bk): Ivan Semenyuk/Sh; 26: MikeDotta/Sh; 27: FooTToo/Sh; 28: Joanna Dorota/Sh; 30: Mari Dambi/Sh; 31 (up): Laura A. Markley/Sh; 31 (left): noprati somchit/Sh; 32 (sun): yusufdemirci/Sh.

Table of Contents

How Can You Act? 4

The Act of Writing a Letter ... 6

Act and March! 14

Acting Makes a Change 22

Glossary 30

I Can Do It Pledge 32

How Can You Act?

The word **act** can mean different things. Sometimes it means what people do in a play.

Act also means using your voice and actions to make change. People act to make sure the world is better.

The Act of Writing a Letter

If you have a pen and paper, you can act! All you have to do is write a **letter**.

You can share your thoughts and feelings in a letter. You can also ask a **leader** to make a change.

The Big Letter

One 8-year-old wrote a letter about the water in her town. Mari wrote a letter to President Barack Obama about the water in Flint, Michigan. It was not safe. It was making people sick.

I Can Do It Corner

Make a list of leaders you know in your community.
- Your classroom teacher
- The mayor of your town
- Your parents

She wanted to **protest**. She used her voice to speak up for herself and her neighbors.

The Big Question

Then Mari asked a big question. She asked to meet with the president to talk about the problem.

President Obama wrote back!

The President's Letter

President Obama said that he was proud of Mari for using her voice.

The president said he would come to her town to meet her. He agreed that something had to be done.

I Can Imagine It

What is something that you would like to change in your community?

Act and March!

You can act in different ways. Mari acted with a letter. Other people might act at a **march**.

A march is a kind of protest. A group of people walk from one place to another. They march to be seen and heard.

Marching Signs

To get ready for a march, people make big signs. The signs show what they care about. The signs have strong words and pictures on them.

Marchers walk with their signs. They are loud. They want others to know what they think. They march to important buildings.

I Can Do It Corner

Draw what your march sign would look like.
- Would it say **PEACE** in big letters?
- Would it tell people to recycle?
- Would it show different kinds of people holding hands?

Black Lives Matter

In 2020, people all around the world marched for the Black Lives Matter **cause**. They saw how Black people were not being treated fairly by police. The Black community asked for help.

People chose when and where they were going to march. They used their phones and computers to share their plans.

Marchers on the Move

People marched everywhere. Even Mari marched for Black Lives Matter in Flint.

Marchers held signs with names and faces of Black loved ones. They said things like, "No **Justice**! No Peace!"

I Can Imagine It

What does **positive** change look like to you?

Acting Makes a Change

Everyone can act and make a positive change. You can do it by yourself or with a group.

Writing a letter lets you share your feelings. It also helps you share ideas for how to make a change. Marching teaches others. You can ask your friends and family to march with you.

Real Change

Mari's letter to President Obama got him to visit her town. The president saw the hurt caused by the bad water. He gave $100 million dollars to help the town.

Leaders saw the people marching for Black Lives Matter. The leaders made new laws. The new laws ask the police to treat everyone fairly.

This Kid Did It!

Greta Speaks Up

Greta was eight years old when she learned the planet was getting warmer. Greta was worried about the future.

She spoke up. Greta gave a speech to over 100 leaders. She told them they needed to do something about the problem. "It is still not too late to act," Greta said.

You Can Act, Too!

Think of something that you would like to change. Find out what leader can help. It might be your principal or the president of the United States!

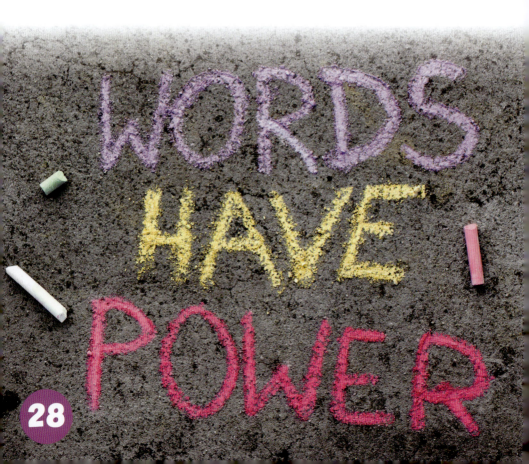

Write them a letter. Tell them:

★ What you would like to change
★ How it makes you feel
★ Why the change needs to happen
★ Ideas you have for how to fix it

If you do not have any ideas for a fix, do not worry! Be like Mari and just ask for a meeting. Then you can come up with an idea together.

Glossary

Act: (akt)
using your voice to make change

Cause: (kawz)
an idea that people support

Justice: (JUH-stuhs)
fair treatment

Leader: (LEE-der)
someone who is in charge of a group of people

Letter: (LET-uhr)
a written message that you give to someone else

March: (mahrch) a type of protest that is a group of people walking from one point to another

Peace: (pees) no fighting or war

Positive: (POZ-uh-tiv) good

Protest: (PROH-test) an action that shows you do not agree with something

I Can Do It Pledge

Now you have read about acting. Grab a sheet of paper and make a sign. Write about what YOU will do. Use this pledge as a guide.

I Can Do It

_____(Your Name)_____ is an I Can Do it Kid!

_____(Your Name)_____ did _____(1 thing)_____

to help __(pick one: self, family, school, community, or world)__

on ____(date)____ be more

(pick something positive: awesome, friendly, full of kindness ...)
_____ .